Wicca for Beginners

Spelling It Out!

Doreen Brown

Copyright © 2011 Doreen Brown
All rights reserved.
ISBN: 1467903019
ISBN-13: 978-1467903011

Table of Contents

Introduction 4

Part 1: The History of the Wicca 6
   1. The Old Ways 6
   2. Modern Wicca 8

Part 2: Principles of Wicca 9
   1. The Goddess & God 9
   2. The Wheel of the Year 12
   3. The Five Elements 19
   4. The Wiccan Rede 21
   5. Tools of the Craft 25
   6. Magic 33

Part 3: Getting Started 36
   1. Meditation 36
   2. Clearing and Grounding Energies 39
   3. Circle Work 42
   4. Natural Magic 48
   5. Divination 67

Part 4: A Wiccan's Grimoire 74
   1. Seasonal Spells 74
   2. Protective Spells 79

Doreen Brown

Introduction

Wicca as it stands today is a revival and recreation of ancient pagan religious ideas, sometimes known as *Pagan Witchcraft*, the *Witch Cult*, *The Old Way* or just simply as *The Craft*. First brought to light in the early twentieth century, Wicca started as a series of investigations by prominent thinkers and researchers into modern folklore, and the pre-existing religious traditions that pre-date Christianity, especially within the British Isles.

Its characteristics include an intensely earth-centred outlook (including a reverence for the natural world, nature worship and the observance of seasonal rites), as well as a belief in the higher spiritual realms of the Goddess and the Horned God – symbols of our essential nature and the principles of life itself. Pagan Witchcraft attempts to tie us back to our beginnings and our belongings, reminding us of where we come from, to what we owe our existence, and placing us within the natural order (rather than opposed to it as in rationalist traditions). For the Pagan all of life is sacred; an expression of the Goddess and the God. It is for this reason that modern Pagans try to reconnect with nature, be aware of what they eat and how they impact the world, consider all of their habits and actions as part of a sacred journey. To find guidance and to connect with the divine force immanent in life most Pagans conduct *Ceremonies*, *Rites*, or *Magic(k)* in which they attempt to manifest the qualities of the Goddess and the God, and bring balance to the spiritual forces at work in their life.

Through the course of this guide I hope to introduce you to some of the key concepts for the Wiccan practitioner, including some of our history, our beliefs and practices. Whilst this is certainly not an exhaustive study by any means, it will arm you with the beginners' tools necessary to start your own investigations into this nourishing and fulfilling spiritual journey. May your journey be long, and may the Goddess watch over you.

Blessed Be

Part 1: The History of the Wicca

1. The Old Ways

There has always been a rich religious tradition in the British Isles, and indeed, throughout the globe. Some of the earliest instances of Cave Art are thought to be religious in application, and burial rites have been discovered that pre-date even this. For untold millennia before the written word ordinary people had a strong and strident spiritual life that referenced the seasons; the natural world; and the forces that are all around us and make up our bodies every moment of our existence.

These pagan traditions formulated themselves through time into religions, and tried to answer the questions that are still of deepest relevance to us today: Who are we? Where do we come from? Why are we here? They offered practical and mystical advice of how to deal with the challenges that we may face, from praying, fasting, beseeching the gods and performing certain duties. They also sought to provide succour to us as we pass through the stages of life; to know what to do when we are young, to when we are starting families, the duties of the parent and the care for the elderly.

Whilst much of what we once knew has been lost because of the lack of written knowledge and the emphasis on the Oral Tradition, many elements of this natural religion persist; in the names of many herbs and plants, in myths and legends, and in architecture and archaeology.

Another reason for the loss of these traditions is the active persecution of the Pagan peoples throughout history by more organised religions. 'Paganism' became associated with 'hedonism' and 'chaos' – even with Satanism, when in fact Paganism was itself a highly diverse and sustaining religious style, and nothing to do with the traditional Christian concepts of 'The Devil' or of 'Evil'.

Little bits of this legacy persisted however and we find it hidden in superstition, in the prevalence of mother-figures found throughout ancient architecture (and even used in early churches and temples). Much of our present medicinal knowledge is based upon the discoveries of ancient herbalists, alchemists and natural scientists (consider for example the plants '*Self Heal'* and *'Ladies Mantle'* whose chemical benefits in the correct preparations are in tune with their names).

For the Wiccan, we try to decipher from these Old Ways the truth and the meaningful, to make use of them in our present situation. The student of the Old Ways is constantly seeking to discover that personal connection to the mysteries of being alive, and uses the old and the new as inspiration and guidance to do this.

2. Modern Wicca

Wicca as it is today is a diverse, ever-evolving and changing discipline. From the early sixties onwards many different traditions began to evolve, including *Gardenerian, Alexandrian, Dianic, Cochrane, Cornish, and Faerie.* At present Wicca itself sits within a large sea of Neo-Paganist thought, with some movements trending towards Old Norse, others to the Celtic Traditions, Breton, Native American Indian, South American, Haitian, feminist, anarchic and countless others.

It is also worth noting that it is just as common to find a solitary witch as a member of any particular lineage of teaching. These developments have opened up Wicca for any serious student, and who needn't be put off by overt tradition.

Green Wicca

Since the Sixties Wicca has also become tied to a growing 'earth-wise' awareness embodied by the Green, Holistic and New Age Movements. Whereas the original members of the Witchcraft revival where mostly academics who broke the boundaries of their time, now the modern Wiccan is more likely to have a strong personal interest in the Earth, in the Natural World, in self-sufficiency, herbalism, recycling and being environmentally aware.

Part 2: Principles of Wicca

1. The Goddess & God

The Triple Goddess

One of the principle beliefs for the Wiccan is the belief in the Great Goddess, most usually in her triple-form of Maiden, Mother, Crone.

The Great Goddess is the Mother Goddess of all ancient peoples, and some variant of her is found throughout the known world, from every indigenous and pre-industrial society. She is at once the Mother of all life, creation, and the nourisher of all beings. In the Wiccan tradition she is especially tied to the natural world and its cycles – harking back to ancient Greece and the true Nature Goddesses of Demeter, Gaia, and Persephone. In South America we are made aware of Pacha Mama; the world goddess who gives sustenance to all things that grow on the land. In Ancient Irish myth we hold reverence for Danu, the Mother of all peoples and 'Queen of the Land'.

Her ties with femininity and the lunar cycle are obvious; she is a progenitor deity who births life from the void, as a parent nourishes and provides for it, as a maiden holds beauty, adventure and attraction, and who is able to scold and guide her creations as a crone. These characteristics are found by the Wiccan also in the new, the waxing, full and waning moon and its connection to the woman's menstrual cycle.

The Maiden -Mother – Crone are seen as primal archetypes that that exist at once as a deity and as forces inherent in the world and ourselves. The Maiden represents mornings and spring, new beginnings, love, innocence, poetry, art and beauty whilst the Mother represents daylight and summer, nature and nurture, marriage, pregnancy and birth, abundance and responsibility. The final force, that of the Crone represents the waning of things, of wisdom and judgement, night-time and winter. The Crone aspect is perhaps the archetype most associated with magic, dreams and initiation. The three forces are stages that we may pass through in our lives, and each exhibits strengths that we can draw on – they also each have their responsibilities and their duties. It is possible to apply these attributes to your activities and your thoughts: at what stage is this venture? Where is this feeling heading, and what is its opposite?

The Great Goddess, as opposed to the Horned God or masculine thought, is seen as an *organic* and *Holistic* deity. Rather than the masculine process of goal-orientation, strength and directed force the Goddess is Queen of communication and community, of drawing things together into their natural place and of overcoming obstacles with an abundance of skills (rather than brute strength). Yet we are also reminded of the great strength of the Goddess in her natural 'Gaia' aspect, as the creator of storms and hurricanes, wind and weather.

The Horned God

The consort of the Great Goddess for the Wiccan is a deity known as the Horned God, who draws on many ancient sources – most notably Greek, Celtic and Egyptian. He is known as the embodiment of the male gender, of the wild, wilderness, sexuality and virility as well sometimes as death and resurrection.

Traditionally the Divine Consort for the Wiccan is symbolised in ritual by the actions of the High Priest, and serves as a focus for those energies. In Irish mythology (the fundamental elements of which are adopted by most of Wicca) the Horned God has a definite life cycle and Mystery associated with him. He is a youth or a light god in spring, marries the Great Goddess in summer (Beltaine), is crowned at Lammas/Lughnasa and ritually dies at Samhain, only to be reborn at the winter solstice and lead the Wild Hunt as a youth on Imbolc (the first of Spring).

Whilst he is a wild god, the Horned God is known as the lord of wild beasts and the Hunt, for savagery, strength, sexuality and the natural order of things. As a sun god, at the height of his powers he is known for skill and determination, for wisdom and 'kingliness'. Finally the Horned God also becomes a sacrificial god – a deity whose mystical strength lies in the understanding that sometimes you have to let go of strength to persevere and sacrifice your goals to the greater good.

The Horned God can be approached especially when in the Wild and through all things wild. Symbolic of Oak, Acorns, rock, hair and Seeds in general, by meditating with these things we can begin to associate with the Horned God. When wanting to commune those abilities and characteristics of the Divine Consort we should consider staffs, rods and wands – as well as asking ourselves what role our strengths and passions play in our lives.

2. The Wheel of the Year

All Wiccans adhere to the Wheel of the Year, which is a celebratory system of interacting with year as it passes, its seasons and changes. For the Wiccan all of life, like the year is cyclical and is endlessly in the process of re-birthing itself. By studying and participating in the wheel of the year we can gain a much deeper awareness of our place in the universe, and become more in tune with who we were meant to be.

The Sabbats and the Esbats

The eight seasonal celebrations for the Wiccan are called the Sabbats, of which four are called the Quarter Days. The Four Major Sabbats are; The Winter Solstice (Yule), The Spring Equinox (Eostre), the Summer Solstice (Litha), and the Autumnal Equinox (Mabon). These Major Sabbats are astronomical in origin, and rely upon the precise time when the sun is at its furthest and nearest points to the Earth. The Spring and Autumnal Equinox are the halfway points between these dates and indicate the time when the changes in the seasons are really starting to occur in a physical way on Earth. There is great evidence that these mathematical dates where known to ancient peoples, as the stones of NewGrange (Ireland), Stonehenge (England), and the Pyramids are all known to align with these exact date and even times!

The Quarter days are the seasonal festivals of mainly the Celtic and European peoples, but have been found to be almost universally replicated in cultures across the world – from Native American, to South American, India, China, the Middle and Far East. For example halfway between the autumnal equinox and the Winter Solstice the Celts feasted at Samhain (the traditional start of their year), whereas in Mexico at around this time we have the Day of the Dead, and even in modern times Remembrance Day (held to remember the fallen of the two World Wars) is held on the first Sunday of November.

The *Esbats* however, are a very different matter, and are more associated with Pagan Witchcraft rather than any particular culture, although the Near Eastern Religions of India, Thailand and Bhutan all also have religious celebrations according to the lunar calendar. The Esbats are known as the Witches moots, and there are 13 every year, one for each moon cycle (and most are held at Full Moon by covens of Witches, with some notable exceptions at Dark Moon). The Esbats are a time for Pagan Witches to come together and celebrate, discuss and learn – this is traditionally an event associated with groups or covens of practitioners to come together and reinforce their development, both individually and as a collective.

Samhain (Oct 31st)

Samhain is where the Year begins. Its new name is Halloween, and is the point that the veils between the worlds grow most thing, encouraging divination. For the Wiccan it signifies the death of the Sun King (or the Horned God) and simultaneously the possibility of rebirth.

Samhain Rite

Samhain is the time when we honour our ancestors and ask for their guidance and wisdom in the days to come. Traditionally it is the day when the veils between the worlds grows to its very thinnest and inspiration can be sought through the TAROT, or any other divination system. Here is a simple Samhain rite.

In the evening of the 31st, when night has fully fallen light a candle, so that it may be seen through a window. Perform your *Clearing* exercise described further on in this book. Gently ask the Goddess for her guidance in your task and remember that all of the wisdom of the world is there waiting for you, and eager to help. As the candle burns, watch its smoke and speak some of your most troubling affairs into its flame. Ask your ancestors and your spirits to give you counsel and guidance in the days to come. When you are done, it is important to thank them by either spreading more light to give them warmth, or having a feast and leaving some of that food aside for the unseen guests. It may be beneficial to leave food outside as an offering, or to place flowers and incense on your altar to honour and please the spirits. When you are done perform the *Grounding* described later in this guide.

Yule, or The Winter Solstice (Dec 21st)

The astronomical point where the sun is at its very farthest from the earth, and thus creates the Longest Night for all of Gaia's children. It is a time to feast and light fires and noise, to welcome back the sun when it passes the midnight and returns to us at dawn – essentially marking the shift in the year as the days get brighter. Perform a celebration (either a Circle or a merry gathering) in which you have a feast of all the years best gains; chutneys and fruit conserves, brewed wines and beers, pickles, syrups and jellies.

Candlemas, or Imbolc (Feb 2st)

It is the Celtic seasonal rite marking the promise of spring. It is asserted that on Imbolc that The Horned God leads the Wild Hunt for the first time, and we celebrate the first births and promises of new growth. This is the time when the Goddess is called back from the Winter with the light from candles and fire, cheer and company.

Imbolc Rite

Imbolc is the time for new beginnings and casting out the old, it is the time that we fully embrace the coming year and think about what we want to achieve. First of all, consider a good spring clean in preparation for the new energies that will soon begin to flood into your life.

Take a white candle, and, placing it before you perform your *Clearing* exercise. This can be further enhanced by the *Awareness Meditation* beforehand. Light the candle and think about the sort of person you want to be and the sorts of activities you want to achieve this year. As you gaze into the aura around the flame (but not the flame itself) silently beseech the Goddess for her powers of inspiration and creativity. It may help you to write some of the aspects of yourself and your life you wish to get rid of this year and, after you have beseeched the Goddess destroy the paper. Bury it in the ground outside, burn it in a fire, tear it up and throw it away. This rituality signifies to your brain that you are now entering the new, and embracing the new person this year will require. Thank the Goddess and, if the candle is still lit, snuff it out. Keep it in a sacred and safe place so that you may light it again to ask for inspiration and insight.

Eoster, or the Spring Equinox (March 21st)

Eoster is when Spring has finally come, and we celebrate the Goddess in her Maiden aspect and we prepare and look forward to all the rewards that our hard work is about to achieve in the coming summer. Consider holding a feast and a celebration for the arrival of spring. Go on a long walk into the countryside and notice the new flowers and stirrings of insects, notice the greening buds on the trees and feel the changes in the air. Best of all for this time of year – go on a Mystery Egg Hunt!

Beltaine (May 1st)

Beltaine is the Wiccan celebration of fertility, marriage, love and virility. Spring has transformed into Summer and the Goddess has taken the Horned God as her consort, the growing year is now ruled over by the Goddess. Beltane is a time to celebrate and make merry and rejoice in your physical selves.

Beltaine Rite

Beltaine is a good time for celebration, romance and marriage. Performing a hand-fasting ceremony, telling your true love what you feel or seeking strength and passion are all good actions to be considered at Beltaine. Here is a simple spell that can be performed for Romance.

Get the freshest apple you can find (preferably picked straight from the tree or scrumped from a friendly garden! Take it home and, before beginning perform your *Clearing* exercise described later in this book. Wash it in clean spring water (fresh mineral water will do at a pinch, but fresh water or rain water would be better). As you wash it consider the impurities, negativities, worries and fears between you and your love being washed away. Next, with your *boline* or a simple kitchen knife carve a symbol into the apple reminiscent of your heart's desire. It could be the first initial of your lover's name, a simple heart, or a symbol that represents what you most want in the world. Next, eat the apple! As you eat it, *really* taste its freshness and goodness, and silently ask the Goddess that she may bring qualities of that freshness and good energy into your love life, or your heart's desire.

Litha, or the Summer Solstice (June 21st)

A celebration of summer's strength, and giving thanks for the crops growing in the fields, the budding fruits and the first returns of an early harvest. It is when the Sun is as its peak. The Horned God gives way to his role as the Sun God of Light and Strength, whilst the Goddess gives way to her Mother archetype. Hold a grand celebration and feast or ceremony dedicated to the strength of the Goddess and the God. There should be games and rejoicing, laughter, song and dance.

Lughnassa (August 1st)

It is the harvest festival when the first returns of the year come in. It is a time to celebrate our hard work and give thanks for the growing earth.

Lughnassa Rite

Lughnassa is a time associated with strength and vitality, and is also traditionally associated with water. Travel to your favourite beach, stream or river. On your journey gather nine smooth flat stones, or alternately nine straight twigs. When you get to your destination take a moment to perform the *Awareness Meditation* described further on in this book. Take in the bright, strong and fresh breeze and lively sights and smells all around you. When you are ready take each stone or twig and cast it into the waters. Each one represents your hopes, wishes and dreams – either specified or generic. Consider using this simple chant as before you cast them:

Three for the past, three for the present, and three for the future.
Three for the Maiden, three for the Mother and three for the Crone.

As each one skims off into the water it carries with it your dreams and your wishes, and is transported to the otherworld of possibility. Have fun and enjoy the act. Play 'pooh sticks' over a bridge or if in company see who can skim furthest!

Mabon, or the Vernal Equinox (Sept 21st)

Mabon is the time of preparation and community. We are aware that the year will be getting colder and we give thanks for what we have whilst making assurances of how to survive the long winter. It is however a happy time when we look to our community and family for happiness.

3. The Five Elements

The Five Elements, symbolised by the five points of the pentacle are the elements which make up all of life. They are based on the ancient alchemical systems and bear strong resemblance to the Indian Ayurvedic System, and the Chinese system of Qi, or *Chi* energy. The Wiccan seeks to balance these five energies in their life and allow each one to enhance the next.

Air

The element of Air governs the wind, and as such it entails quick thought, dynamism, new ventures and horizons. It is the Ruler of intellect and rationality, and its symbols are the sword, dagger, *athame* and knife.

Fire

The element of fire represents our passions, our intention and Will as individuals; creativity, productivity and strength. It governs all ventures where are our interests are piqued, and its symbols are the rod, wand and staff.

Water

The element of Water is representative of our emotions and our subconscious, our feeling selves. It governs our romantic and our intuitive selves, and its symbols are the Cup and the Sea.

Earth

The Earth element symbolizes physicality, practicality and durability. It Rules over all physical things – our bodies and our environment, and is associated with the facts of our material being: our history and our ancestors. Its symbols are the Rock, stone and the Square.

Spirit

The element of Spirit is, in essence, ones true self; as it should be and as they are in the eyes of the Goddess. It is associated with all the spiritual senses of the soul; psychism, divination and the oracular. It is often represented by the individual themselves in rituals as they 'embody' their beliefs and actions in this life.

4. The Wiccan Rede

The Wiccan Rede is perhaps the only 'guidebook' necessary for Wiccans. Its full version (repeated below here) encompasses all the essential teachings and beliefs of how to practice. You'll notice the law of the elements and the seasons, as well as the essential Tree Lore all contained within its verse.

The Rede encapsulates what it means to be a Wiccan, and forms the underlying ethical framework from which we all operate. It can be shortened and memorised as a mantra into these timely words:

*Bide within the Law you must, in perfect Love and perfect Trust.
Live you must and let to live, fairly take and fairly give.*

These Eight words the Rede fulfil:
"An Ye Harm None, Do What Ye Will"

The Role of the Witch

The modern Wiccan or witch performs a very special function in today's society. Just as in yesteryear the Wiccan acts as Priestess and Priest, Healer, Sage, and Counsellor. If you feel that you are drawn to this faith consider yourself in these functions, and how you would help the earth around you.

The Wiccan as Priestess/Priest

The Wiccan holds a very special role, one who is actively seeking communion with the Goddess and the God, and ever striving to be closer to the essential truth of our existence. As such you may be called upon to impart your wisdom and skills for the service of the Goddess. Your deep respect for the Earth, for the sacredness of all things and awareness of the cyclic nature of existence gives you the responsibility to speak out to defend your Earth, the Great Mother, your Community and Family.

The Wiccan as Sage

You may be called upon to give wisdom, do readings (divination, psychic or TAROT) or perform a magical act. Through your studies and hard work you will find that you develop skills in these areas and others will recognise that too. Weigh up each offer as to its merits, intention, and final outcome. The work of the Goddess should never be sold cheaply and never treated as a commodity. You will have to consider if the person asking you to perform the magical act or divination is trustworthy, honest, or greedy and self-interested. If you are ever approached to curse another or bring ill fortune to another than you should part company with that offer immediately as it goes against the Will of the Goddess and acts as a magnet for negative energies.

The Wiccan as Healer

The true role of the children of the Goddess is that of the Healer. It is our duty to balance negative energies, to further life and abundance. You may find yourself as time goes on being drawn to such causes such as environmentalism, animal welfare and conservation, you may become involved in looking after people's hurts or giving advice. The best advise that anyone can give you on this journey is that the effective Healer is someone who knows who to heal themselves; whom to turn to when they need help, and when to call a stop to imbalanced actions, activities and thoughts. Through this rigorous self-knowledge your healing skills will begin to percolate through to the people who need it most around you.

Tarot for Beginners: Your Future. Now!

The Full Rede:

Bide within the Law you must, in perfect Love and perfect Trust.
Live you must and let to live, fairly take and fairly give.

For tread the Circle thrice about to keep unwelcome spirits out.
To bind the spell well every time, let the spell be said in rhyme.
Light of eye and soft of touch, speak you little, listen much.
Honor the Old Ones in deed and name,
let love and light be our guides again.
Deosil go by the waxing moon, chanting out the joyful tune.
Widdershins go when the moon doth wane,
and the werewolf howls by the dread wolfsbane.
When the Lady's moon is new, kiss the hand to Her times two.
When the moon rides at Her peak then your heart's desire seek.
Heed the North winds mighty gale, lock the door and trim the sail.
When the Wind blows from the East, expect the new and set the feast.
When the wind comes from the South, love will kiss you on the mouth.
When the wind whispers from the West, all hearts will find peace and rest.
Nine woods in the Cauldron go, burn them fast and burn them slow.
Birch in the fire goes to represent what the Lady knows.
Oak in the forest towers with might, in the fire it brings the God's insight. Rowan is a tree of power causing life and magick to flower.
Willows at the waterside stand ready to help us to the Summerland.
Hawthorn is burned to purify and to draw faerie to your eye.
Hazel-the tree of wisdom and learning adds its strength to the bright fire burning.
White are the flowers of Apple tree that brings us fruits of fertility.
Grapes grow upon the vine giving us both joy and wine.
Fir does mark the evergreen to represent immortality seen.
Elder is the Lady's tree burn it not or cursed you'll be.
Four times the Major Sabbats mark in the light and in the dark.
As the old year starts to wane the new begins, it's now Samhain.
When the time for Imbolc shows watch for flowers through the snows.
When the wheel begins to turn soon the Beltane fires will burn.
As the wheel turns to Lamas night power is brought to magick rite.
Four times the Minor Sabbats fall use the Sun to mark them all.
When the wheel has turned to Yule light the log the Horned One rules.
In the spring, when night equals day time for Ostara to come our way.
When the Sun has reached its height time for Oak and Holly to fight.
Harvesting comes to one and all when the Autumn Equinox does fall.
Heed the flower, bush, and tree by the Lady blessed you'll be.

Doreen Brown

Where the rippling waters go cast a stone, the truth you'll know.
When you have and hold a need, harken not to others greed.
With a fool no season spend or be counted as his friend.
Merry Meet and Merry Part bright the cheeks and warm the heart.
Mind the Three-fold Laws you should three times bad and three times good.
When misfortune is enow wear the star upon your brow.
Be true in love this you must do unless your love is false to you.

These Eight words the Rede fulfill:
"An Ye Harm None, Do What Ye Will"

5. Tools of the Craft

The Magical Tools for the Wiccan are very important, but not essential for entrance to the faith. They serve as focuses for our Will when we are conducting ceremonies and magic(k), directing our magical energy and announcing to the Goddess our actions. As such they are considered sacred, but the actual type of object may vary from practitioner to practitioner. For example it may feel 'right' to you to have a full, ceremonial knife to only be used at magical workings – whereas others may favour a pocket blade that they can carry and use as needed.

Setting up an Altar

The Altar is the central element for the Wiccan faith. It is where you honour the Divine, perhaps conduct the mysteries, and remind yourself of your dedication and the essential truths. It is common for every Wiccan to have a corner of their home dedicated as an altar, perhaps also an altar in a separate ritual space, and for others it is necessary to be able to quickly set up an altar wherever they are to conduct their mysteries.

The altar should be a holy and a sacred space; it is your physical connection to the Goddess and the God. Many Wiccans choose to decorate it with figurines of the mother goddess and the horned God, as well perhaps as their particular deities, ancestors, and spiritual allies. It is also customary to keep your Tools near, in or on the Altar, as well as offerings to the divine. Current motto's and reminders, current spell workings and projects are also included into the altar space. It is, in essence a material manifestation of your magical self.

Decorating the Altar

1. Choose something that symbolises the Triple Goddess, wither three unique things, or one thing that is reminiscent to you of her qualities. In the past I have seen the conjoined three of pine seed cones, goddess figurines, or three bowls.

2. Choose something that symbolised for you the Masculine and the Horned God. This could be a figurine, a particular two-pointed piece of oak, an acorn, or stone.

3. Think about the allies and influences that are important to you, have formed you into the person that you are today, and whose wisdom you seek to guide you into the future. These could be family members, ancestors, guru's, teachers, symbols, flowers, stones or pictures that represent to you their teachings. On a Buddhist altar I have often seen a leaf skeleton that reminds the monks of the Buddha's teaching of impermanence.

4. Think about your beliefs and the forces you wish to bring into your spiritual life. Use objects, art, things of natural beauty that symbolises them – in particular it may be worthwhile including a pentagram in some form or another.

5. Decorate your altar with beauty, honesty and intent. Think about other religious ceremonies and places of worship and think about including; scented candles, incense (and holders), crystals, models or beautiful pieces of craft, garlands of flowers, symbols of the natural world, art. Your altar will change over time, and will reflect your interests and your spirit, as well as your current workings.

Cleansing Your Altar

- When building your altar consider using a large piece of stone or wood as a base – something solid to represent the base of your Craft. Spend some time cleaning, cleansing and sanctifying your altar space.

- Build your purest intent into your altar space, chant, hum, or pray your secret wishes to the Divine whilst you create it.

- Cleanse your altar often. Wipe away old incense, clean oil burners, remove used and old (undesired) decorations and objects. As you do this, remember that you are undertaking a sacred act, and you are making a place where the Divine can manifest itself into your life. Consider cleaning your altar every lunar month, or before every Sabbat.

Privacy and the Altar

- Remember that your Altar is a Holy centre, and whilst it is not universal - it is interesting that many sacred things are also secret. It should be a place where you whisper your deepest hearts' desires, your secret fears, and your hidden courage. Don't throw these special parts of yourself to the public or to be squandered by others who may not understand.

- Your Altar should also be a place where you can be undisturbed whilst you conduct your rites, prayers and blessings. You may prefer this to be a hidden place, or perhaps your alter is something unobtrusive?

- Altars are not always necessary grand affairs, but the more intent and impact it has then it is generally true the more it will occupy your life as well. There are some Wiccan's who also carry altar elements with them wherever they go, so they can find a quiet space and set up an altar when and as they need to.

Choosing Tools

Your Tools are the objects with which you conduct your spells and your ceremonies. They can take a number of forms but the most common are listed below. You may also find that objects – some of them everyday – become magical tools over time as they begin to be more associated with your magical work, or take on deeper significance. You should always consecrate your tools before you use them, and when in use your tools should be as appropriate as possible to the ceremony or spell. This means that the feeling of the

Tool and the function for which you are using it for should match as closely as possible. Think about your intent and what you are using it for, what the Tool means to you, what direction, element it might remind you of. These are all ways that will make your spiritual development more effective.

Pentacle

The pentacle is the symbol of the Wiccan faith, and is depicted by the five-pointed star inscribed on a disk (traditionally wood or stone). This is a grounding object and serves to capture energies, grounding the user and as a protection from negative influences.

Associations: The Element of Earth, Protection, Strength.
Colours: Brown, Earth and Umbar

Athame

The athame is traditionally a black-handled knife that is used to inscribe candles, carve runes, or any magical act that describes your magical thought. It can serve as a pointer, and has a martial aspect – so use it when you want forceful, cunning action (although blades are also associated with workmanship, medicine and skill).

Associations: The element of Air, Thought, the Will, Intention.
Colours: Blue, Black, Grey

Wand

The Wand can be a simple twig that catches your interest and 'feels' right to you, or an elaborate creation with handle and decoration. It should generally be the length of your hand and a half, and harvested by you from a wood that you feel a strong connection with. It is used to 'zap' magical energy, to control and direct the flow of magical will and is a powerful focus.

Associations: The element of Fire, Inspiration, Passion, Creativity.
Colours: Red, Orange and Yellow

Cup

The Cup (or chalice in some traditions) represents the element of water, emotions and memory, and the feminine. It is symbolic of our mysterious inner subconscious, as well as our flow of feelings and should be used when working with emotions. The cup itself, just like the water element has powerful regenerative, self-sustaining and healing connotations.

Associations: The element of Water, Feelings, Healing, the Female.
Colour: Blue, Slate-Grey, Sea-Green

The Book of Shadows

The Book of Shadows is a term used to describe your magical journal, or diary. It is a book within which you note down your magical experiments, important events, inspirational quotes and pictures, thoughts and musings. It should be a record of your journey and your interaction with the Divine. Keeping the Book of Shadows is nigh essential for a Wiccan, as it allows you to look back over the seasons and years and detect trends, themes, strengths and weaknesses in your work. Review it a few times a year, and reflect upon how you are writing, what you were going through at that time in your life, where you were heading and where you are now. Use these insights to guide you in the present. As a scientific and an inspirational document the Book of Shadows charts the realms that you are investigating, and can give birth to new careers, artistic endeavours, poetry or writing, and your personal history. Note down the results of all your magical endeavours, and your rites and ceremonies. Write secret love letters to your inner deities and tell new myths to your future self.

Associations: Wisdom, your Spiritual Self.

Wicca Cards

The cards are a form of TAROT which are designed for divination and spiritual growth. They operate as a guidebook and a system of self-illumination to help the budding Witch decipher problems, analyse situations and receive inspiration. Split into four suits (Wands, Cups, Pentacles and Swords) they correspond with the four elements (with yourself representing the Magical Link, the element of Spirit). Use them to describe your path in this manner.

Wands- problems and answers with relation to your spiritual journey.

Cups – problems and answers with relation to your emotional life, your past and your feelings.

Pentacles – to be used about your home environment and work life, any aspect of your physical self.

Swords – Answers pertaining to your will, thought and dynamism. Any area in which your force (your directed energy) is battling a situation.

The Major Arcana, or the Picture Cards let you develop your intuition, and can serve to reveal hidden currents underneath your life's journey. When facing a difficult situation, ask for the Goddesses blessing and pick a random picture card. Meditate upon that symbol and decipher what the image is trying to tell you about your situation, where you are heading and where you have been.

For further ways to use the Cards and the Tarot, see the chapter Getting Started with further uses for the TAROT and Divination Techniques.

Associations: Wisdom, Spirit, Knowledge and Inspiration.

Other Tools

A Wiccan will have many tools for their use, and consider some of the following for their effectiveness and scope of application. The important thing to remember with any tool is that it serves a purpose for your spiritual self. Almost item, memento or keepsake can become a tool as long as it attains relevance and importance for you.

The Bell – To invoke spirits and to purify an area.

The Besom – A broom to brush away unwanted energies.

The Boline – A small, single-bladed knife used to cut herbs and carve wood.

The Sword – A martial weapon used in ceremonies of high import to 'knight' and name, to cast out negative forces.

The Staff – A tall walking staff as high as the shoulders which is made from an especially significant wood, used in protection, travel and wisdom spells. Ideally you should make your staff yourself, from one of the Tree's listed in the Natural Magic section of this book. A good starting staff can be made from stout Ash, Hazel or Thorn.

The Candles and Lantern – Different coloured candles or a simple lantern which serves to purify an area and in wish-offerings and dream-imaginings.

Consecrating the Tools

Each Tool should be properly blessed and consecrated before use. This involves the item being made or taken individually and given into the service of the Goddess. There are a number of ways you can consecrate each tool: by incense (smudging), by burial, or by washing.

When we smudge, or use incense we hold the item or the sage smudge stick and pass it through the smoke of our sacred incense (usually frankincense). As we do so we beseech the gods to look over it, to bless it, and to use it in their service and guide its user.

When we bury an item for consecration it is placed before sunset in the ground, wrapped in a strong cloth with an appropriate colour for the item. Or alternately use a white cloth, tied securely around the item with string. This we leave in the arms of the Goddess and the God for a whole turn of a day, before returning roughly 24 hours later to unbury it, wash and use.

Washing involves washing the item gently with natural spring, mineral or rain water. This removes any impurities and negative influences and makes it holy and ready for use.

Consider using the following words alongside your consecration ritual:

> *Light of the Goddess, God of the Wild,*
> *Accept this Gift from your Child,*
> *Let it do your Work, fill it with Strength,*
> *From you to me, it is thus Lent.*

6. Magic

Magic is the act of transforming your Will into reality, or causing change in accordance with Will. For the Wiccan, magic is at one and the same time a sacred and an organic act. By this we mean that magic – or transformation – is everywhere and all around us at all times. It is the changing of the seasons, the metamorphoses of the caterpillar to butterfly, the process of one thought leading to an emotion and transforming into action.

Magic is also the province of the Witch, who performs it to aid her community and develop herself as an individual. The Wiccan never performs magic to harm people otherwise they would not be a Wiccan, and following the sacred words of the Wiccan Rede.

Magic can be performed almost over every act as we find deeper layers of meaning and try to negotiate the forces therein. For example you might be about to start a new job; you could consecrate this new venture by performing a simple ceremony with your athame (thought) and the pentacle (earth, the material), including an invocation to the Goddess to guide and watch over this work, and invite helpful energies (and/or spirits) to be drawn to this project and to aid you. This announces your intent, focuses your Will, and draws the spiritual energies in an effort of Will.

There are, broadly speaking three types of magic generally performed by Wiccans which fall into the following categories. Some Wiccans tend towards some rites and not others, and some are more 'seasonal' rather than 'evocational' – a good Witch however, has a grounding in all of them as they all function to support and strengthen your activities in the other areas.

Celebration

The magic of the seasons, of the Wheel of the year, the rites of passage and the rejoicing in the Goddesses and God; the celebrant performs seasonal rites at the proper times to honour themselves, their bodies, their community and ancestors, as well as the Gods. Celebrational magic informs our life's path as we change through the seasons and years and fixes our goals.

Evocation

The magic of evocation is a broad term to refer to anything that *evokes* a force. This force could be a spirit or elemental, an emotion or quality, or even the Goddess and God themselves. It is the bread and butter of magic, and describes any act where we try to balance the energies or influence the outcome of an act.

Examples of evocation are the enchanting or runes into ones workspace to further study, the casting of love spells, the calling for spiritual guidance (bringing those forces into our life), healing, casting out demons and negative influences, healing the earth, calling on divine inspiration in the many forms of divination.

Ceremonial

Ceremonial magic is perhaps the least practised of the Wiccan magical rites as it usually entails a group and an ordination into a particular tradition of Wicca – although also a group of magical friends can also conduct a ceremony! Ceremonies are designed to raise a lot of energy and to mark very important events, such as initiations and rites of passage within a tradition, or a declaration of one's devotion to the Goddess, but they could also be the choosing of a magical name or the naming of a child, a marriage or handfast, a funeral or wake.

Within the ceremonial space we use a lot of associations particular to the task at hand and the individuals involved. This informs our subconscious of what we are doing and focuses our magical Will. For example a naming ceremony might be held in a grove of trees particular to inspiration and guidance (Rowan, Birch, Elder, Ash); it might also have flags to convey the spirit of Air and our thoughts being carried into the otherworld. Special robes may be worn, and special incenses used to symbolise intent and personality. Then the designed ceremony begins...

Part 3: Getting Started

1. Meditation

Meditation is one of the foundational skills that the Wiccan needs to gain some experience in. The benefits of meditation are numerous and generous: from self-awareness, poise of spirit, relaxation and a deeper communion with our spiritual selves.

Of the many ways to meditate, here is listed a good beginner technique that will help you develop on your Wiccan path.

Awareness Meditation

This simple meditation aims to increase your awareness of yourself, create a connection between you and your environment, and is a good start for any further meditation, magic or spiritual work. It can be performed at any time of day, and almost anywhere – but its benefits when it is performed at the very start of your day are greater as your conscious mind and the worries of the Ego haven't fully kicked in. It charges you and prepares your mind for the spiritual aspect to life. Through this meditation you may come to learn things about yourself and your emotions, about what is troubling you and what is sustaining you.

1) Begin by being seated, lying down or standing. When you get practised you can perform this meditation even when busy, when walking or performing routine tasks.

2) Take a few deep breaths in and out, and with it release the tension that we all have been subconsciously holding throughout our days. Take a few moments doing this.

3) Try to imagine your muscles and tensions ebbing out of you, like waves or a tree shedding dew. It may be helpful to visualise a white light slowly spreading throughout your

body, from crown of your head to the tips of your toes as your body and your mind relaxes.

4) Make an internal note as to your intention for this meditation, that for this moment you are setting aside time for this practice, that this practice is sacred, and you need not be worried by little upsets, anxieties or confusions. Your mind will bubble away thoughts about your life, what you plan to do and what you have done, but as long as you just let it play out and you gradually reaffirm that you are letting it do its thing it will begin to quiet.

5) Open your eyes and breathe regularly and calmly. Be aware of the sensations of the breath, its tastes and smells as it flows into you and out. Spend a few minutes doing this.

6) While you are still in a calm state, take a gentle notice of the sights, smells and sounds around you, just noting them, letting them go and thinking no more of them. Try to inhabit the present moment and not get caught into investigations or speculations about what you see, feel, hear or smell. Listen to the breeze and the weather, the faint sounds of birds or insects, the passing of people going about their daily lives. What season is it? Is it Winter with the tang of freshness in the air? Can you taste spring on the breeze? Make no judgements.

7) Next note what you see, again in that non-judgemental frame of mind. Soon you will find your awareness blossoming of your surroundings, picking up on the tiniest of sensations near and far.

8) Be aware of what you are feeling, physically, mentally and emotionally. Again make no judgements, just note what is happening, what your train of thought is telling you, how you feel. You may discover deep seated worries or anxieties, or deep sources of joy and contentment.

9) Finally, and with purpose, reflect that everything that you have experienced, and everything that you are is a manifestation of Life itself and the Goddess. It is all justified by being in existence, has a part to play in the transformation

of life from one state to another, and as such, is sacred.

10) Give thanks for this experience to the universe around you, and when you are ready, come back to your normal awareness. Allow yourself some moments to readjust and 'wake up' once again.

2. Clearing and Grounding Energies

A lot of the work performed by Wiccan's can be described as Clearing work, and is one of the reasons why many Witches also have as a part of their ritual apparatus a *besom* or a broom made of a stout wooden shaft and twigs. The *besom* is used for the symbolic clearing of unwanted energies in a space.

There are many variants on Clearing and Grounding, and as a technique can vary in application from feeling energised to a whole-scale healing (removal) of negativity. Clearing and Grounding, alongside Meditation are three of the most useful skills for a witch to be practised in.

Clearing

Describes the removal of unwanted energies, and, like washing a sheet returning to a natural state. Clearing should always be performed at the start of any magical (and indeed, spiritual practice), whereas grounding should always be performed at the end. Here is a simple exercise to perform clearing on yourself and your surroundings.

1) Attain a relaxed and alert state of mind – this can be done through the Awareness meditation described in the previous section.

2) Focus your intent and make your declaration, do this by stating a few words of meaning to you which can vary according to your particular beliefs and intent, but here is an example:

> *Goddess Watching Over Me, God At My Side,*
> *In this Grace, I Abide,*

Doreen Brown

*By Light and Life, Rock and Weather,
May The Goddess Bless This Sacred Endeavour*

3) As you speak the words imagine white light spreading down from the heavens into you, your body and your surroundings. As it passes through you it leaves you feeling revitalized and refreshed, and soon it reaches your feet. Imagine your toes digging down into the core of the Earth and finding sustenance there as a tree does, and drawing that wholesome energy back up into your breast. It might be helpful to imagine it as a deep living green force which brings with it joy, strength and courage. It may help as you negotiate these energies to draw your hand down your body as the white light of inspiration and blessing floods down, and then, when you are ready, draw both of your hands up and clasp them at your breast as the living power of the Earth fills you.

4) Spread your hands out in front of you (if you are using a wand it may help to sweep it ahead of you as if casting a stone across a lake) – as you do this imagine some of that energy overflowing, cleansing and energizing your immediate surroundings. The negative influences you carry and the ones in your surroundings are cast out and transformed by the healing white light of the Divine and the wholesome energy of the Earth.

5) Clasp your hands back together over your breast, sensing the beat of your heart and the pulse of the Goddess and God therein. Feeling satisfied, clean, stable and alert thank the Goddess.

Grounding

Grounding is the process of returning to ones normal state of awareness, and is absolutely essential for any magical participant.

Tarot for Beginners: Your Future. Now!

There are many witches and adherents out there who have suffered burnout, magical paranoia and delusions of ego because they repeatedly failed to ground themselves after altered states of consciousness. Grounding is, in essence, a means of quieting down those senses which we are generally unaccustomed to – our sixth sense, our heightened sensitivities, latent psychism etc. It is necessary to return to a normal, functional 'self' because it allows the information and energy that you receive during magical work to filter through your subconscious, and gradually become assimilated. The dangers of forcing yourself to take too much on, experience too much too quickly are well documented.

1. Take a few deep breaths and clear your lungs. Wait until you feel a little more restful, composed and at ease. Don't particularly try to achieve anything or think of anything – just relax.

2. Under your feet, imagine a bright pentagram – the symbol of protection. Into it pour all the unwanted tensions and energies. Feel them leaving you, leaving behind a more relaxed and at ease person than before. The Pentagram flashes three times, once for each goddess and slowly fades back into the earth.

3. Slowly bring yourself back to normal awareness, open your eyes and clasp, clap or rub your hands together as if washing them in air. Feel the sensations of skin on skin and the reality of your body. Shake your limbs a bit as if after an intense exercise, bringing some blood back into your legs and arms.

4. Forget about it! Work out what you have to do next with your day – as normal and mundane as it may seem and get on with it. It could be going shopping, having a wash, chatting with friends. The important thing is to leave the magical space behind, be done with it and move on with your activities. The magic you have performed will still be working away in the unseen realms, and is in the hands of the Goddess now and you do not have to think about it anymore!

3. Circle Work

Wiccans often perform their ceremonies and particularly the seasonal and more important rites within a circle, and is sometimes called Circle Work or Circle Magic. The are used for any endeavour which requires greater power and deserves deeper respect than quick-cast magic.

The circle is an ancient symbol of wholeness and unity, and serves to symbolise a microcosm of reality. That means to say, that whilst in the circle the Wiccan sets about describing the universe, and then seeks to call upon forces inherent within it. The first step is Casting The Circle, into which we must Raise Power.

Decorating the Circle

The Wiccan first picks a good spot for her magic. This is preferably outdoors, under the trees and with all the natural elements present: wind in the trees, good earth underfoot, maybe the sound of water afar. If they so choose the Wiccan can decorate the circle, this serves as a visual reminder of the different forces and elements at play, and is also an offering to the Divine forces; as always – any act of Beauty is also one of magic.

Casting the Circle.

They then define the circle by either imagining or physically defining the boundary. Slowly turn around full clockwise whilst imagining a bright line starting from the east and extending around you to south, west, north and back to east. As you do this, imagine the blessings and the power of the earth filling this space. It might be helpful to throw a pinch of salt as you walk the circle to purify it.

Calling the Watchtowers.

The Wiccan then calls the elemental forces (or Watchtowers in this context) to bear witness and enter the circle, to empower it.

The East

The Wiccan turns to the Eastern-most point in her circle and points with her wand (or it may be more appropriate to use another of the ritual tools, depending upon the 'feel' and intent of the ritual). Imagine a strong, stiff breeze blowing in from Eastern quarter, carrying with it promise and adventure.

The South

Turning respectfully to the south, the Wiccan repeats the gesture and, answering she imagines the hot warmth of the southern wind flood into the circle, bringing with it strength and excitement.

The West

Continuing with the circle the Wiccan invokes the powers of the west, imagining a salty, sea breeze entering the circle from that direction bringing with it memory and passion.

The North

For the final Watchtower, the Wiccan repeats the process and the gesture and invokes the powers of the North. Its associating wind is cold and stern, and brings with it the smell of earth and rocks laden with minerals.

Raising Power

The Wiccan must raise power into the circle, to make a light worthy of the elemental forces and the Divine. This also serves to imprint the occasion upon their subconscious and to fully activate all of the magical senses. Raising power can be done in a number of ways, and is generally achieved when everyone feels excited, alert and confidently joyous. Here are a number of ways in which the power can be raised:

Chanting

With a series of words pre-designed by everyone (or just for the witch alone) the Wiccan chants as many names of the Goddess that they know, in a formulaic fashion and memorised by heart. Alternatively the Wiccan may chant Maiden, Mother, Crone, Maiden, Mother, Crone and repeat until they feel happy and joyous and alive with strength.

Drumming

A steady beat is best to be used, before gradually speeding up and raising the tempo and passion as you feel the energy begin to build.

Dancing

Dancing alone or in a group, with or without music can be best for raising power. Dance around the edge of the circle, skip your feet and hold one hand into the sky like a child. Complete this circuit at least three times before, giggling and joyous return to your place in the centre.

Treading the Circle

Probably the most performed by solo witches, the Wiccan begins by walking slowly once around the circle, and then the second time at a faster speed, before third at a jog. If you are practising in a group make sure everyone is holding hands!

Shouting

Starting as a low murmur, everyone (or the witch alone) just repeats nonsensical sounds, or even a simply Om or HUM sound. This they garble and repeat, gradually raising their voices until they are speaking loudly, just as the shout gets to a full throated roar the Wiccan stops, cresting that energy into themselves and the ritual about to be performed.

Invoking The Goddess and the God

Now, with circle complete and feeling strong and joyous the Wiccan attends to the Gods. At the altar they lay an offering reflective of the deity they are seeking to invoke. If it is a ritual designed with parenting in mind than the mother goddess would be appropriate, consider using lambs wool and fruit. For the Horned God consider a special bit of wood, some fresh acorns or smooth stones. The offering should be special to you, and reminiscent of the deities and the task at hand. Many times people use feathers and flowers to signify their wishes, supplications and beauty of the Earth Mother.

Internally or aloud, speak a blessing and ask for their guidance in this magical work. This part of the rite should be a sacred, subtle and reverential, full of quiet joy and tranquility. The simpler and more heartfelt this supplication the better.

A Simple Blessing and Invocation;

Great Goddess I beseech, I am your child, May your guidance and blessings bring light to this endeavour...
Great God of Wood and Wild I beseech, I am your child, and may your strength and wisdom bless this endeavour...

The Rite/Ceremony/Ritual Itself

What happens next inside the circle is up to you who designed it. If you want to seek guidance you may just silently pray or call on the attributes of the Goddess to flood into your life. If you wish to bless a new venture you may ritually burn a note or a plan to signify those desires travelling into the otherworld in the form of smoke. If you want to get rid of a difficulty it may help to speak your fears to the divine, write them down and throw them into a fire to give them away.

Imagination is key when designing and performing ceremonies. You must clearly define what you want to achieve and set about a simple action which describes that. If you want to seek new love you may bury a heart-shaped rock or a seed into the growing and sustaining earth. A ritual may involve a mummer's play, re-enacting scenes from the great myths, it may involve dancing, singing or any group activity. It may also be about invoking (evocation) of forces, of imbuing items with certain properties so they may serve you as reminders of your faith, bring you good luck and courage. When doing this use the any appropriate runes, symbols and images for your task. The more you describe and feed your task with symbols the more it will key into your subconscious and allow your magical self to work at it, hidden, over time. In time you may develop your own magical 'language' of symbols for the elements, for love, hope and family, or for qualities such as moving forward, remaining strong, encapsulating wisdom. All of these are beneficial and useful for the Pagan Witch.

Closing the Circle.

When the Rite is performed the Circle must be closed before we leave it. This involves thanking the forces and ritually 'breaking' the circle and allowing its energies to flood out into the universe and begin the work that you have asked them to do.

Thank the Goddess and God, any spirits or ancestors for their help. Raise three cheers and throw your arms into the air, be joyous. Thank the quarters, each in turn (beginning with the North, and heading to West, South and finally East. Thank them either silently or loudly, but with heartfelt conviction. Finally, the Witch breaks the circle by drawing a line across the threshold in the air, and exiting.

Merry Meet and Merry Meet Again!

Generally what happens after Circle Work is that the group involved start rejoicing, good humour and food and drink are all imbibed and seek to return the individuals back to their normal, physical selves (similar to *Grounding*). If you are a solo practitioner, consider going out and meeting up with friends, or going for a walk and having some food.

4. Natural Magic

A large aspect of any Wiccan's path is their relationship to the natural world, reverence for its cycles and taking advantage of its wisdom. Indeed, it could be said that as the children of the Goddess we are duty bound to investigate and understand the world around us.

A New Understanding

Often for many people when they start to undertake the Wiccan journey they begin to see themselves and their surroundings in a new way; an outlook of reverence and awe for the life around them and inside their own breast. As each phenomena becomes to be understood as a manifestation of the Goddess, we see that each phenomena has its part to play in the cycle of life, and has its own mysteries and lessons to teach us. The plants we encounter on the wayside – be they the sudden unfurling of a spring wild flower, or a meeting with a grand old tree, even the weather and the flights of birds can take on a new significance. This understanding does not cease just with the natural world, but extends to your encounters and your daily habits as you begin to see the energies of the Divine at play all around you.

This is one of the reasons why many Wiccans take great care to understand the natural cycle, the names and the hidden meanings of the plants and animals, the stars and the planets. There are many ways open to you into this new understanding of the magical universe; it could entail a study of folklore and superstitions, an understanding of your own health, the rhythms of what you eat and expose yourself to, or the powerful magic of growing things in your garden from seed to fruit. Below is a short introduction to some of the lore of the natural world that you may find useful in your daily journey, to help and heal and to attain wisdom.

Herb Lore – A Wiccan's Kitchen

Herbs and plants are a good way to enhance your spells, to evoke for rituals and practically to heal your body. They can be considered natures gifts, and each have their own magical correspondences which tells us the most beneficial times to use them, and how.

Evoking With Plants and Herbs

Evoking with Herbs allows us to use the plant's energies to enhance our rituals and magical work. Collect some of the plant and let dry on a windowsill over the course of a day and night, keep well ventilated. Preferably collect wild where you can or from a plant that you have cultivated yourself. Never take the whole plant, but a handful of cuttings, always bear in mind the size of the plant and it as an organism as well – pay reverence and say thank you to the plant.

When the plant has dried a little sprinkle some in a circle around your ritual space or altar. Alternatively use it as a 'throw' which you cast out in the four directions when you honour the elements and the sacred directions. Choose the appropriate plants for each direction/element.

Offerings and Blessings of Herbs

Actually a very old practice, evidence of offerings and blessings being made of plants can be seen in the Harvest Festivals where a sacrificial harvest loaf is made, and even in a brides bouquet – traditionally a collection of thirteen different plants and herbs which are called to 'bless' the bride.

As above, collect and prepare some of the wild or cultivated plant with respect and care. Take to your ritual space or altar and place at the central point as an offering to the Goddess. You can specialise your choice of Herbs to a particular Deity, or choose herbs which embody the qualities you wish to bring out in your magical self. As a blessing, consider giving a collection of the herbs to a worthy person, or use the plant as a blessing for your home.

Herb Bags

One of the best and easiest ways to use Herbs and plants is to create Herb Bags, which are little sachets of the dried plant material which will slowly exude its energy to you over time. For best results use Herbs which have strong natural oils within them, enhancing the smell and thus the impact of the spell.

As above, collect and prepare the preferably wild or home-cultivated plant, providing care and respect to the plant and the Mother Goddess as you do so. When the plant material is dried, crush, crumble or chop in fine fragments and place in a small sachet (no bigger than three or four inches, and tie or stitch shut with a piece of cotton. For best results make the bag yourself out of some material which is slightly gauze-y like muslin, to allow the smells and fragrance of the plant to seep through. As you put your bag together consider the qualities that you are asking to enhance your life and your magical working.

Carry the bag with you, or put it under your pillow for one lunar month (from the new moon to the following new moon, or from full to full moon). After this period, thank the Goddess and the Divine and find a safe, out of the way spot and bury the bag to return it to the earth.

Baths, Oils and Teas

Many of the herbs and plants listed below can be used as essential oils, tinctures and teas. Consider using aromatherapy oils in your bath to enhance your well being, and drinking appropriate teas at certain times of day to enhance your clarity of thought and vigour.

Any good health food shop will be able to advise you on the medicinal uses of herbals baths and herbal teas.

A Sacred Bath

Before an intense ritual working – wash yourself thoroughly – you are about to interact with the Divine, and Cleanliness is Next to Godliness, as some may say! Gather to you these essential oils and prepare your bath before your magical working. These oils will stabilise and deepen your bodily energies, preparing you on a psychic level for the task ahead.

Add 3 Drop Frankincense, 2 Drops Sandalwood, and 3 Drops of Lavender Essential Oil to a hot, steaming bath. Let cool for a while before bathing.

A Wiccan's Essential Herbal:

Lavender

Element: *Air*
Ruler: *Masculine, Mercury*
Has strong cleansing and antiseptic qualities, a few drops of the essential oil on a pillow or in a bath will ease worries and troubles. Suitable for calming and clear thought. Stimulates the immune system and also acts as an anti-depressant and as a protective against negative forces. The flower spikes are used primarily, although the leaves can be used alongside. Consider throwing into a fire on a Sabbat for its purification and healing properties, and is often used alongside powerful healing spells.

CaoCao (Chocolate)

Element: *Water*
Ruler: *Venus*

CaoCao is a very ancient and sacred plant, used by the Aztecs and the Mayans in the Day of the Dead festivals to honour those who have passed away. It is a powerful aphrodisiac and stimulant, and is used best as an offering to the spirits, for good fortune and in love spells.

Daisy

Element: *Water*
Ruler: *Feminine, Sun*

The Daisy is a beautiful herbal reminder of the Triple Goddess and Nature in general. It is a strong, courageous and optimistic plant and encourages us to seek our blessings and to remember what good we have all around us. It is strongly protective for women, children, innocence and purity in general. As a love herb the common daisy can be made into chains and signifies pure and loyal affection. As a wisdom herb the Daisy can be used to access the fairy realms, and as a promise from the healthy spirits that populate the otherland. It can be used in wishes and dream spells.

Clover

Element: *Air*
Ruler: *Feminine or Masculine, Mercury*

Clover (and in particular Red Clover) is beloved by hares and rabbits, which are sacred animals to the Goddess. They are also in the good – luck associations linked with the world of the faerie, the otherworld and of sight.

Clover is a powerful symbol of good luck and good fortitude, as a symbol of fortune it encourages courage and optimism, and new beginnings. It is associated with the Triple Goddess and the promise of wisdom. Thought to be a protective for women, and an encouragement for men to take heart in good luck.

Sage

Element: *Air*
Ruler: *Jupiter and Venus*

A powerful cleanser, Sage is used in smudging ceremonies to ritually cleanse a space. As a medicinal herb Sage is used as a throat gargle to cleanse the mouth and throat of infection and thus it can be understood to 'speak clearly' with sage. Sage is essentially a blessing herb, and used for health, vitality and the seeking of beneficial wisdom.

Rosemary

Element: *Fire*
Ruler: *Sun*

Rosemary is an antiseptic and a mild stimulant, and is often used in cooking to aid digestion. It is a herb with the properties of the Sun and the God within it, as it encourages healthy appetites, longevity and vitality. Rosemary can be used as an 'active cleanser' when you are out doing magical work, encouraging a dynamic and vigorous good will when used to evoke or scatter in a work space.

Comfrey

Element: *Water*
Ruler: *Saturn.*

Comfrey is a powerful healer and a 'method' plant. Its creams and poultices are often used for deep sprains and broken bones, and comfrey is thus associated with the processes and the foundations of things. Linked with the Crone aspect of the Triple Goddess, the comfrey gives wisdom to those who seek it, and seeks to strengthen structural change in ones magical life. Comfrey is a good protection and dedication offering.

Mint

Element: *Air*
Ruler: *Mercury and Venus*

Mint (commonly known in its forms as peppermint and spearmint, but actually the mint plant has many different varieties) is a mental stimulant and cleanser. It is especially good for clear thought and for protective magic when you need to be able to ward off negative impulses and have simple, straight forward thought. Mint should be used *after* a ritual working or in grounding or clearing spells.

Ginger

Element: *Fire*
Ruler: *Mars*

Ginger is a strong stimulant and digestive aid; used to activate the nervous and immune systems. In Chinese Herbalism ginger is seen as a fiery herb and is good for warming the client and giving them a zest for life. Ginger can be used as a source of courage and to enhance a strong, protective atmosphere. As a tea or in digestion ginger is a good preparation for a long or complicated ritual working.

Wiccan Tree Lore

For the Wiccan, the trees that surround us are very powerful living entities, whom we should pay our respect to as fellow denizens of the planet, and whom can guide us on our spiritual journey. Trees have often been associated with mystery and magic, and have been found to be included in the Ancient Celtic Ogham (or calendar and writing system) of runes. The Ogham in particular references every lunar month with a particular tree, and a 'time' in which that tree is king – a practice that is strongly reminiscent of the progress of the Horned God and his Lady as they travel through the Sacred Year.

Tree Wisdom can be used to help our magical workings, and used as guides or allies in the pursuit of wisdom. Consider getting to know some of the trees in your area, from the largest specimen to the hedgerow shrub, consider the oldest and the young saplings around you as trees are often planted at sacred and special places – at way stones, crossroads, meeting points, churches and wells. It was considered incredibly unlucky to chop down the singular tree in the middle of a field as this was the Faery Tree, or the home of the fey who looked after this patch of land. The biggest and grandest tree in a copse too, is considered to be the Mother Tree by many traditional cultures across the globe, and looks after and is home to the spirits who protect that domain.

Using Trees in Your Magical Workings.

There are many ways to use trees as a Wiccan. The simplest and best is to get to know your local trees, and when you have a special affinity go every few days and sit by its trunk, watching the tree as it grows and changes according to the seasons. Its strength, patience and generosity can teach us a lot about the flows and energies of life.

Other ways include; *Divination, Protection, Healing.*

Tree Divinations.

Select a rod (or wand) made from a single stem of a tree branch. Never take from a young tree, and always ask before you cut. This rod should be no more than a foot, fairly straight and should speak to you of the tree which is its parent. You may decorate it, carve, sand and protect it how you wish. Use the rod either a wand in your magical workings or 'cast' it in Divinations. See how it lands, especially if you are casting a group divination with a number of tree wands; consider what its movement in the air and on the ground means to you.

Protection.

Place your tree wand (see above) about your door, entrance or exit to where you are, quietly ask the spirit of the tree to protect your home. Trees are renowned to be strong and virile creatures, with some of the strength and perseverance you are trying to impart to your home. Alternately a tiny piece of tree back, leaves or seeds can be carried by the person as a reminder of that trees qualities, and to call on its energies when you need them most. Remember that you should always be respectful, ask and give thanks before you use any part of a tree.

Healing.

Either use your tree wand (see above for the creation of the wand) in your healing spells, using the appropriate tree for the appropriate spell (for example oak for strength and courage); or alternately you can find the trees whose qualities you think would be good to imbibe for healing and, in the reverential frame of mind ask it for its guidance and help in healing a particular ailment. Consider spending a few hours with the tree as you gain its energy and its wisdom.

A Wiccan Tree Almanac:

Alder

Elements: *Water, Air*

One of the sacred trees in Druidry, the Alder represents healing and wisdom.

Apple

Elements: *Fire, Earth*

Another sacred tree to the Druids, the Apple represents fertility and abundance, and is especially used in love and good fortune spells.

The Apple bestows a loving, giving energy and thus is a good way to access the Nature Goddess.

Ash

Elements: *Fire*

Chosen by the Druids for its straight and true grain, Ash makes the best choice for wands for this reason and its close association with fire, the Will and psychism. Generally considered a masculine Tree and a Tree of initiation.

Birch

Elements: *Water*

The Birch tree is recognised for its strong feminine associations and was in old times called 'The Lady of the Woods' – for this reason consider using it's leaves in love spells, or the healing of any emotional hurt. A gentle and recuperative Tree.

Blackthorn

Elements: *Earth*

The blackthorn is a common hedgerow shrub that produces strong and dangerous thorns during the year, and then fruits sloes in the autumn and early winter (which make an excellent preparation in Sloe Gin). The Blackthorn is sacred to the Crone aspect of the Triple Goddess, and is thus associated with fate, finality and judgement.

Broom

Elements: *Air*

The Broom is a small shrub – type tree used especially in the making of the Witches Broom or besom. It has a strong ritual healing and purifying connotations, and using it to make a ceremonial broom to sweep the ritual space is considered one of its best uses.

Cedar

Elements: *Earth*

The Cedar tree is renowned for its concentration and abundance of cedar oil, which is especially connected with all things mortal: from death and ending ceremonies, to the practice of grounding. To ground and centre yourself after a magical working, consider rubbing your hands with a few crushed cedar leaves.

Elder

Elements: *Fire*

The Elder tree (also known as Elderberry) produces flowers that can be made into wine, and berries that can be made into jams and pickles. It is a sacred mother tree, with strong associations with midsummer, the otherland and the faeries. The Elder tree is generally thought to be a Wisdom tree, and is also known as Old Mother Elder. A wand made from her branches is especially useful in working magics, enchantings and dream work. Consider going to the Elder tree at midsummer to commune with the Other Realms.

Elm

Element: *Earth*

The Elm is a hardy and strong tree with a tan bark and a very fibrous wood which makes it resistant to splitting with an axe. It is thus known as representing the Strength of the Goddess and shows her displeasure for being used for firewood. The Elm, because of its strong structural qualities, is excellent for adding stability, grounding and fundamental protection to your magical endeavours.

Fir

Element: *Air*

The Fir is a hardy tree useful for when vision and clear thought is needed. It is a tree that stands in high places and looks over vast distances, and even in the hardiest of circumstances still grows. As such the fir is a good regenerative tree, able to bring healing, hardiness and endurance to those who ask for it. Consider using fir needles when the winter is close or when you have a long journey ahead.

Furze (Gorse)
Element: *Earth*

A low-lying, shrubby type of tree that covers hillsides with ease, the Gorse has a delicious coconut scent to its flowers in the summer, and is a strong protective tree. Use especially at the spring equinox, burn to provide protection and to frighten evil spirits.

Hawthorn
Element: *Fire*

The Hawthorn is a small tree that bears thorns in the year, white May blossoms in spring, and red berries that can be specially prepared into jams in the autumn. The Hawthorn is a very noble tree of the Other World, love and marriage. When the May Blossoms first appear, consider your passions, desires and interests.

Hazel
Element: *Water*

The Hazel is also known as one of the Faery Trees, because of its usefulness in magic, protection and psychism. A Hazel wand is thought to be very beneficial, and lends itself to noble magics and healing. The Hazel is a beloved tree of the Goddess, and is used to provide protection to any and all that as need it.

Holly

Element: *Earth*

The Holly Tree is one of the Sacred Druid Trees, associated with the Winter Solstice, the secret promise of the Goddess to return and the rise of the Horned God. The Holly is one of the only things that is green in the depths of Winter. The Holly is thought to be very magical, useful for ascertaining truth and honesty, and associated with protection, healing, and the endings of things.

Juniper

Element: *Air*

The Juniper tree is known for its berries and its strong aromatic oils, and was considered by the Druids to be a good protective tree of house and home. The Juniper tree is said to be able to bring visions, and protect the home against negative influences, thievery and bad luck.

Mistletoe

Element: *Earth*

The Mistletoe, with its red poisonous berries is the other sacred Winter Plant for the Druids', and is a powerful protective plant. It is a masculine symbol and useful in virility, love, and rejuvenation spells.

Oak

Elements: *Fire*

Known as the 'Forest King' the Oak has strong connotations of the Horned God, and was sacred to the Druids for its longevity, its strength and endurance. Consider making a wand out of Oak for its discrimination and kingly powers, and its long-lived wisdom.

Almost all parts of the Oak, from Acorn, leaf and wood can be used in a magical working.

Pine
Element: *Air*

The Pine has been known for its purification and cleansing action for thousands of years, when Pine needles were burnt to purify cattle and the home. As a tall, straight tree the Pine brings to mind clear sight and clear thought. Consider scattering pine needles around your ritual space, your home or work place to ritually purify it.

Rowan
Element: *Fire*

The Rowan is one of the sacred trees to the Druids, and is thought to be very magical. It has a delicate appearance and red poisonous berries that each bear a pentagram in their shape. Rowan is a good choice for a wand, and an excellent divination tool.

Willow
Element: *Water*

The Willow is associated with flowing water, with inspiration, dreams and healing. Spend a few hours under a Willow to receive insight into your dreams and desires, and beseech the tree when you are in distress and in need of healing.

Yew
Element: *Earth*

The ancient Yew tree, long planted in graveyards (and many pre-dating the churches that sit besides) is a deep magical tree of death and rebirth. Its berries are poisonous and Vikings used to bury their funeral sacraments in Yew casks. The Yew regenerates out of itself, and so is thus never truly dead. The Yew is a strong Earth associated tree, and reminds us of our ancestors.

Wiccan Sacred Stones

A Wiccan's natural magic doesn't include just the plant kingdom, but all of nature. As such the Wise Wiccan draws inspiration and Wisdom from the animal kingdom, movements of the weather, and the mineral kingdom as well. How can we not when some of our oldest spiritual places in the world are standing stones and monoliths! The practitioner of Wicca tries to reconnect with what ancient people as a reality: that even the mineral kingdom was an expression of divinity, and it can be used to enhance our spiritual life.

Stones obviously play a big part in ritual and ceremony, as many stone circles are aligned with the Winter and the Summer Solstice. It is thought that stones, with their crystalline structure can refract and focus energy, capture information and act in a similar way to the Earths own acupuncture's needles in the theory of geodes. A Wiccan generally always has a passing familiarity with the stones in her landscape, and often keeps special sacred stones or crystals about her person to be used when the magic is called for! Below is a simple list of some of the most effective crystals that can be used in a practical and daily way by any aspiring Wiccan.

Cleansing and Keeping Your Crystals

Your Crystals and ritual stones should always be kept as pure as you can, for despite their hard surface are actually very sensitive objects which take on the auras of their environment easily. Every time you buy a gemstone it should be cleansed before use – especially as it has been handled and been sitting in a shop for some time! You can forgo this step for natural stones you find or pull out of the ground, but all of your sacred objects – no matter what they are – should be cleansed once in a while, depending upon frequency of use.

To cleanse them you can bury, smudge or wash crystals. Wrap them in a simple cloth and bury them overnight (somewhere you can find them again!), letting them take in the natural goodness of the earth. If you are going to wash or smudge gentle bathe them in sage smoke or clear rainwater, speaking these words with a clear heart as you do so;

> *Goddess Three*
> *and God of the Tree*
> *I ask your blessing on these,*
> *Make them bright and whole,*
> *pure of intent,*
> *Only Light and Good is meant*

Healing With Crystals

To conduct a healing with a crystal, place your chosen stone on the affected body part, or draw a human on a piece of paper and place the stone over where is being affected. Let its energy saturate into that part whilst you meditate, opening your spiritual senses to help the flow of the energy. Imagine the stone or crystal glowing its associated colour and slowly filling that body part with its colour. When you feel that the work is done, take the crystal away and thank the stone, the God, and the Goddess for their help. Finally, ground and clear any leftover energies!

Evoking With Crystals

Stones can be used in a ritual way to call upon their associated forces. Use them when you set up your ritual space by placing them in the corresponding sacred directions or alternately placing them at your altar. As you do this, breathe clearly and imagine gently bands of pure light filtering into the stone and projecting it into the sacred space like powerful lasers. Each beam adds to your ritual space the energy it is affiliated to. When you are finished and closed your circle it is important to clean and cleanse your crystal to 'tune it down' again after such a sacred and intensive use!

Artemis', Clusters and Rounds

Many crystals that are available to buy come in one of three types; the straight wand of the Artemis, the multi-pointed 'cluster' and the smooth pebble-like Round; each has different uses and excels at different tasks.

The Artemis is especially useful as a wand, for directing energy and pinpointing the energy flow, whereas the cluster is better used for cohesive harmony and problems with multiple facets. The Round is especially useful as a pocket stone for subtle workings, and for comfort and support magical workings.

A Wiccan Crystal Toolbox;

Amethyst

Ruler: *Spirit, West, Venus*

The purple amethyst has been known for its spiritual and psychic associations, especially in the production of medium-ship abilities. A general stone of good fortune, the amethyst can be used any time a deeper spiritual awareness is needed.

Aventurine

Ruler: *South, Mercury*

The green aventurine is a positive and lucky stone, said to bring good fortune and to be especially useful in contacting the otherland. A useful heart stone, said to promote both physically good health in ones heart and in ones emotions.

Carnelian

Ruler: *Sun, South*

The red and orange carnelian is a powerful blood tonic, and is useful in grounding energies into the physical realm and promoting physical health.

Clear Quartz

Ruler: *Any Direction*

Clear Quartz is especially useful in protection and protection of the psychic centres. A good cleanser which promotes clear thought and positive clearing energy.

Flint

Ruler: *Mars, Thought, Earth*

Flint, although an abundant stone is one of the oldest known tools used by our species – as arrow heads, blades and axes. As such it is incredibly useful for directed action, thought and motivation. As a reminder of our ancestors Flint can be used in ancestor worship and its special 'elfbolts' are used in connection with the fairy lands (see below).

Granite

Ruler: *Earth, Jupiter, North*

Another abundant stone, granite is notoriously tough and durable, and reminds us of our past and of endurance. A piece of granite could be used to ground energies or as a statement of direction and perseverance.

Moonstone

Ruler: *Moon, West*

The Milky moonstone is a particularly powerful psychic tool, used to induce visions and receive inspiration from Or Lady of the Stars. Should always be covered and cleansed when not in use.

Rose Quartz

Ruler: *Venus, West*

The pinky-red rose quartz is beneficial to all forms of magic to do with the development of ones heart and its emotions, your romantic life and forgiveness. The Rose quartz, like all in the Quartz family is about clarity and purity.

Tormaline

Ruler: *Saturn*

Inky Tormaline is a stone of grounding and powerful protection which acts as a magical negator: able to disenchant and stabilise an area of its psychic static. Not essentially a healer or a purifying stone, but very useful when quick grounding is necessary and iron-hard protection!

White Quartz

Ruler: *East, Moon*

The White quartz, which is freely available in the ground is a very lucky stone, and represents inner guidance, luck and inspiration. A beneficial and cleansing atmosphere.

5. Divination

When we think of Pagan Witchcraft, one of the images that comes to mind immediately is probably that of the fortune teller, the wise woman, or sage. These archetypes hold relevance for the Wiccan, as they reveal some of the ways in which the Old Religion kept alive its traditions and uses through the long centuries.

There have always been wise people to whom we have turned, be they teachers, guides, guru's or fortune tellers. The Wiccan, with his or her specialist skills in communicating with other realms is in one sense an explorer, in another a doctor of the unseen. The Wiccan retrieves information from the unseen (the Divine) and puts it to good use in their lives, for the benefit of the Earth and their community. Divination is one such useful tool that the Wiccan should be practised in.

Stealing Fire, or Acquiring Wisdom

Divination is the art of *seeing* what others cannot. In one sense it is a form of psychic ability, and in other it is a form of mental and emotional intuition. To the Wiccan Divination is both of these things and is also an act of communing with the Divine. There are many forces and energies at play in the universe, and the Wiccan seeks to understand them; recognise patterns; see shapes of events and trends when they are still in their infancy.

A good way of describing it is smelling the weather. Have you ever walked out on a brisk day, taken a deep lungful of air, noted the colour of sky and thought – *ah, rain is in the air.* Or have you ever seen a conversation between two people and thought there was much more under the surface? Your subconscious mind takes cues from the energies around you in your environment, and, if you are skilled, can recognise that energy and see where it is heading. This is the science of Divination. Another form of fortune – seeking particularly open to the Wiccan is that of the Divine Inspiration or *Awen* to the Druids. This is when the adherent has trained their mind and body to attune itself to the patterns of their deity and has asked for help. Artists and scientists call these phases *purple patches*. Suddenly inspiration, clear vision and knowledge comes to you as facts suddenly *add up*, slot into place and make sense. As a Wiccan it is wise to cultivate your relationship to the Divine and the methods we use to seek it to encourage the *Awen*.

Methods of Divination

There are many methods of Divination available for the Wiccan, and here are listed some the techniques which have proved to work for many.

- Reading the TAROT, or Cards.
- Crystal Ball Scrying.
- Reading the Ogham, or Runes.
- Ink or Water Scrying.
- Dreaming.
- Weather Watching.

As you will see, most fall into two categories, that of Reading or Scrying.

Readings

Readings are generally more associated with tradition tools of prophesy (the Cards, the Ogham, the I Ching etc), and involve you understanding the broad web of associations, clues and references within that system. For example I may randomly pick up a card which is the Two of Swords. I understand that Two represents binary opposites, and swords represents struggle so this could refer to a conflict or contest of wills. Two is also the basic number that we need for human interaction, so I might infer there is a conflict between two people. Two is also a Divine number, representing the

Male/Female opposites, so within this card, although is contest and struggle is the promise of union and joint harmony.

The more you learn as a Wiccan about correspondences and meanings the more accurate your readings will be.

Scrying

To Scry means essentially to 'see', not necessarily with your actual vision (although sometimes this happens!), but more often with your inner eye, your intuition and your imagination. You can train your ability to scry through the art of creative visualisation.

When the Wiccan Scry's they are at first glances watching the water; the opaque depths of the crystal ball; the patterns of the clouds or the movements of the trees. On the inner level they are letting their mind relax and gather the minute shifts in information and allowing the visions blossom in the inner realm. They may become suddenly aware of colours, words, faces or feelings. Development of this skill allows the Wiccan to piece together stories and find hidden truths, and requires a lot of discernment to be able to quieten their own ego and foresee not what they want but what is alluded to in the situation.

An Introduction to Card Reading

The Wiccan Cards, or TAROT are a common form of one of the Witches Tools. Here follows a brief guide to how to use them. For more information, consult my other book ***The Beginner's Guide to the Tarot***.

Cleanse Your Cards

It is essential, before you use them and before every reading that you sanctify and cleanse the cards. This can be done with a variant of the clearing and cleansing rituals described in the Getting Started Chapter of this Book.

You may like to have a specific dedication ceremony for your cards, one which purifies it of any residue energies, and sanctifies it to the service of the Goddess and God.

- Perform a Clearing ritual upon yourself and your Cards. As you do this, hold the cards in your hands and make the gestures (down the body with inspiration and up the body with vital energy) with the cards in your hands.

- Place the cards in front of you on the earth or on a table. Gently waft over it some incense or crushed herbs (consult the Natural Magic section of this chapter for ideas on Trees, Herbs and Crystals to use for their cleansing effects).

- Imagine the white, pure energy you have evoked pouring into the cards, filling them with the power of the Divine, blessing them, protecting them and say these words;

    These Cards I dedicate to the Service of the Light,
    May all who seek it, find its inspiration and might,
    May it bring guidance and understanding,
    by the Goddess and God's Blessing.
    So Mote It Be

- Bring yourself back to your normal frame of mind and begin using the cards.

Ground Your Cards

It is very important to ground yourself and your energies every time after you use the Cards. This can be done with the Grounding ritual described earlier in this chapter, and it may be beneficial to use any of the Herbs, Tree's, Crystals and Tools mentioned in this book. One of the important facets to remember is that you cover the cards with a cloth, and *put them out of sight.* This is the physical representation of changing your mode of thought, and allowing the wisdom and magic that you have sought to continue to operate in the inner realms. Bring yourself back to your normal states of awareness by chatting, eating, laughing.

Understanding the Cards

For a greater analysis of each card's meaning and sample layouts, consult my book The Beginner's Guide to the Tarot, for here my purposes will be to give the aspiring a crash course in the essentials about the cards!

The TAROT is split into two Decks, the Major and the Minor Arcana. The Major Arcana tells us about our life's journey and reminds us of archetypes that we might embody or encounter in our journey. The Minor Arcana is really a descriptive system of all the different sorts of challenges and good fortunes that we may face every day, and is further split into four suits; the Wands, the Cups, the Swords and the Pentacles.

The Major Arcana

0 The Fool - *New Beginnings, Naiveté, Purity*

I The Magician - *Skill, Magic, Thought*

II The High Priestess - *Intuition, Understanding, Psychism*

III The Empress - *Marriage, Fertility, Nature*

IV The Emperor - *Strength, Force, Kingliness*

V The Hierophant - *Wisdom, Religiousness, Proclamations*

VI The Lovers - *Love, Romance, Duality*

VII The Chariot - *Travel, Force, Plans*

VIII Strength - *Strength, Joy, Health*

IX The Hermit - *Wisdom, Aloneness, Research*

X The Wheel of Fortune - *Luck, Fortune*

XI Justice - *Law and Order, Legalities*

XII The Hanged Man - *Martyrdom, Perseverance, Sacrifice*

XIII Death - *Endings, Finality, New Beginnings*

XIV Temperance - *Patience, Endurance, Sagacity*

XV The Devil - *Ill Fortune, Addiction*

XVI The Tower - *Ill-Laid Plans, Bad Judgement*

XVII The Star - *Hope, Inspiration, Luck*

XVIII The Moon - *Psychism, Intuition, Dreams*

XIX The Sun - *Health, Vitality, Vigour*

XX Judgement - *An Accounting*

XXI The World - *The Completed Project, New Horizons*

The Minor Arcana

Wands - *Inspiration, Any Creative Endeavours, Your Passions*

Cups - *Feelings, Emotions, Romance, Memories*

Swords - *Contest, Struggle and Conflicts*

Pentacles - *Material World, Employment, Physicality, Financial Matters*

An Introduction to Weather Scrying

A simple form of Scrying is Weather Scrying, and is commonly practiced by us all when we were children... What does that cloud remind you of? What images can you see? As a basic technique it can be applied to the use of the Crystal Ball, a mere of water (better with a drop of ink swirling within) or tea leaves.

- Perform the Clearing ritual described in the Chapter, and consider using Herbs, Trees, Stones or Tools to help you. A very powerful aid to this type of Scry is a feather you can use as a wand, before letting it go and letting it drift away.

Tarot for Beginners: Your Future. Now!

- When in a relaxed state, perform the Awareness Meditation described in this Chapter. As you near the completion of this meditation, start to shift your focus solely to the sky.

- Retaining that relaxed, non-judgemental state of mind let your imagination blossom in accordance with what you see. It is best to have a clear question in mind which you are trying to Scry the answer to.

- Look at the shapes of the clouds, the fast and the slow movements. The sudden twitching of the leaves and trees, the flights of birds or calls of animals. Remember what type of bird, tree or animal and gently consider what they represent to you – how they move and what they sound like: joyous, optimistic, like a baby's call, a roar, or a promise.

- Images may bloom in your mind's eye, or people, sudden words, memories. Consider them all as they relate to other things you are seeing.

- Feel the weather – is it cold or warm? Windy or still? Is there a change coming in the weather or is it calm?

- When you are ready, come out of your Scrying daze and write your inspirations down. Then perform the Grounding ritual described in this Chapter. It is very important to Ground, and if need be Clear your energies and return to a normal state of awareness!

Part 4: A Wiccan's Grimoire

1. Seasonal Spells

Winter

Ingredients:

One Red candle
One Cup of Spicy Tea, Strawberry, and Cinnamon are good (Mulled Wine will suffice!)

The purpose of this spell, to be performed at any time of the winter season, is to align yourself closer to the elemental forces of the season, and to learn from its wisdom.

Before you begin take a few moments to perform your Clearing Ritual, feeling energised, relaxed and poised. When you feel ready, place your red Candle at your altar space and light it. Say the following words;

> *Horned God of the Wild,*
> *Our Lady of the Earth,*
> *I honour your gifts, both harsh and mild,*
> *please bring to me and my loved ones both light and warmth*

Sip from the cup and watch the play of light from the candle over your altar. Let your mind remember all good memories and fond thoughts about your friends and family at this difficult time of year. You might like to write a simple blessing or prayer for any elderly relatives or acquaintances that you know. Take pleasure in the warm drink and feel its spice sizzling on your tongue.

When you feel comfortable, happy and at rest thank the God and Goddess sincerely for their aid. You may wish to keep the candle burning through the evening or night (being sure that it is safe to burn where it is).

Spring

Ingredients:

Paper and a pen.
A piece of cord of string

This spell is to be performed at any time throughout the spring season, and is designed to keep you attuned to its wisdom and its benefits. It can even be performed once a day during this time of the year, and will only benefit your appreciating of the natural cycles.

To begin with perform your Clearing ritual to feel energised, relaxed and poised for the task ahead. When you are ready, go to your desired spot and begin. This may be a tree outside in the wilds or your garden; or by your windowsill if you live in a city. The important thing is to feel the breeze and the clear air moving about you.

Begin by speaking this invocation into the breeze;

> *God of the Wild and Goddess of the Land,*
> *Take these Wishes and Thoughts from My Hand,*
> *If they Serve to Suit, Keep them Safe,*
> *Let no problems, mar their Way!*

After speaking this write a simple wish, desire on a scrap of paper and tie it with the cord to the tree, your window sill, or some high place where the Wind can get at it. It is wise for these wishes to be ones that you can achieve, and this spell works best if they are plans and ideas for action – imagine them as seeds which you are planting, fed by the winds of life.

When you are done thank the Goddess and the God, and the Wind for their aid. You may find over the next few days solutions to your problems start to arrive, and avenues for you to explore appear unexpectedly at your doorstep! Or you may find that your ideas develop, change shape and encourage you to further action!

Summer

Ingredients:

A quiet few minutes in the sunlight
The purpose of this spell is to help you become attuned to this season, and can be performed at any time or numerous times during the summer.

To begin with, perform your Clearing Ritual until you feel at peace, energised and that your spirit is poised. When you feel ready, begin.

Face the South and the Sun – remember not to look directly at it, but rather feel its warmth on your skin and your face. Speak this blessing;

> *Loving Goddess of the Sun!*
> *I ask for your strength and you're healing to come!*

As you say this raise both your arms and hold them out in a beseeching, joyous blessing to the Sun's power and its vital strength. After all, it is the source of energy for an entire planet! Lets the waves of light flood into you, bringing with it health and vitality; imagine it strengthening what is weak; glory in its abundant joy and happiness.

When you done and you feel positive and joyous, thank the Goddess, the Earth and the Sun.

Autumn

Ingredients:

A paper bag
Some time to find an Oak tree

To begin with, as with any of these spells you should perform your Clearing ritual so that you feel ready, energised and you feel that your spirit is poised. The purpose of this spell is to align yourself with the elemental powers of Autumn, to ask for their benefit in your life and to understand the passage of the seasons. It can be performed at any time or numerous times through this season.

After you have performed your Clearing Ritual set out on a quest to find your Oak tree in mid – to late autumn when it is dropping its acorns. Carry your paper bag with you and have few if no other objectives in mind.

Gather for your bag a number of acorns, do not think over much about which ones or how many – just continue until you feel that you have done enough. Take your bag to a special, safe place or carry it home and sort through the acorns. As you do this, recite these words;

> *By the Power of Our Lady, and the Wisdom of our Lord,*
> *I ask for these things to Ward,*
> *Keep the Good and throw out the Bad,*
> *And with it my worries and thoughts to be had!*

As you sort through your acorns take out all the broken ones, the ones which are rotten or have holes in them – where small insects have burrowed into them! These you should cast away into a nearby stream, hedge or piece of scrub. As you do reflect that, just like these acorns you are casting out your bad habits and the things which are keeping you ill, down or simply aren't useful any more. Keep the good acorns. These are representative of all your strengths, and the things that you have worked hard to gain and create over the year. These acorns should be put to use – you could plant them, feed them to the birds, prepare them for acorn coffee, or keep them as future charms.

You should never exhaust a supply of acorns, and always give back to the Earth something of what you use and take – this could be in the form of growing the acorns from seed, or by returning to look after the parent tree! Look to any good website or book on the cultivation of trees for more in depth advice of how to be a tree husband.

2. Protective Spells

For Good Fortune

Ingredients:

One Gold Candle
Seven Green Candles
Sandalwood Incense

Perform your Clearing Ritual before you begin. You should start this ritual in a relaxed, alert and optimistic frame of mind. Place the gold candle in front of your Altar, and the seven green candles in a circle around it. Light the incense and let its generous and bounteous nature flow into the room. With solemnity, light the gold candle, and then proceed sunwise (or clockwise) to light the green candles around the altar.

As you light the green candles imagine each one bringing in a spark of light, luck and prosperity into your life, the energy flowing from your altar and your gold candle out and into the green, calling to it all good things.

Say these words;

> *Smile of the Goddess,*
> *The Light of Jupiter,*
> *Make for me Happiness,*
> *Fortune and money to Prosper*

Gaze into the aura around the gold candle for a few moments, imagining you're Needs (Financial, Emotional and Spiritual) but not you're Wants. When you are done, blow out each candle in turn, starting with the last one lit and cycling back to the gold. When all the candles are out thank the Goddess and perform the Grounding Rite.

Keep the gold candle and the seven green together and safe (perhaps tie them with a cord) for when you may need to perform this spell again. Most importantly – forget about it! You may be pleasantly surprised at what exactly suddenly crops up in your life – from finding unexpected money to a new friend

Finding What Was Lost

Ingredients:

One fairly long piece of ash twig
One piece of cord

To begin this ritual you must first perform a thorough a Clearing of yourself and your surroundings. There are always stray energetic elements at play in any environment – little wisps of thought or vibration from passing people or encounters which could interfere with the spells direction.

Think about the object in question, and try to have a clear mental picture and feel of it in your mind.

Cast a circle by using your wand to recognise the four quarters, East, South, West and North. Say as you do this;

> *Eastern Powers I Recognise You! Bring to me clear thought!*
> *Southern Powers I Recognise You! Bring to me your passion!*
> *Western Powers I Recognise You! Bring to me your calm!*
> *Northern Powers I Recognise You! Bring to me your memory!*

As all the powers come together recognise that they are each part of the whole, and that you form the fifth element, that of spirit. Nothing is unconnected or is lost.

Take your ash twig and break it in two. Bury one piece in the Eastern corner of your circle (only lightly bury, with a smattering of soil over it. Take the other piece of ash, and, holding it in your hands think about what was once hidden to you. Say these words:

> *May the Goddess Return to me that which was lost,*
> *May nothing remain hidden,*
> *So Mote It Be*

Gently uncover the ash tie you buried and tie it to the one you are holding in your hand with the piece of cord. Consider that all things are never truly lost, and all things are connected as you remember the object.

Thank the Goddess, and thank the quarter elements for their aid, thanking and dismissing them in turn from North to West, South, and finally East.

Perform a thorough Grounding Ritual and set about finding your object!

Keeping Hidden

Ingredients:

A Piece of Cloth
A Small (hand held) Mirror
A single White Candle

First perform a Clearing Ritual to energise yourself and to prepare for this spell. When you feel ready, attentive and energised, begin.

Place the candle on your altar space, before any image or iconography associated with the Goddess. Place the mirror in front of it, facing towards you. Look at your reflection in the mirror and light the candle, note how its light throws your face into shadows and relief. Say the following incantation;

> *Light of the Goddess and Strength of the God,*

> *Hear my plea and let others see me not,*
> *Keep what is Sacred in Your Embrace,*
> *Let No foolish minds cross my ways*

As you finish, cover the mirror with the cloth so none of its surface (and your reflection) can be seen.

Thank the Goddess and the God in any way that feels appropriate to you, and blow out the candle.

Unveiling – After you allotted period it is very important for you to unveil your image from the mirror. Perform the simple ritual again, but this time, after you have lit the candle ask for the Goddess and the God to light your way and your place in the world;

> *Light of the Goddess and Strength of the God,*
> *Illuminate my place, back to where my path was trod.*
> *Let all things return to what they once were,*
> *And let me not be hidden from all good things – near and far!*

This is a very powerful spell, and should only be used wisely. It is worth remembering that sometimes you can be hidden from things which are beneficial to you, or to which need your help. So always remember to unveil and to Ground this spell after use.

Spell of Protection

Ingredients:

Athame or Wand (Ash or Thorn preferable)
Possible Inclusions – Clear Quartz, Hazel, Crushed Ginger, Salt

This is a general spell of protection, to be used at any time when you feel the need, to ward off malign influences, bad luck or aggression. It is a fairly straight forward spell but which can be elaborated upon to turn from a solitary practice to a group enchantment or even exorcism. Turning this spell into a Rite would mean incorporating more elements like the ones I have listed at the start of this spell, for their beneficial properties.

To start this Spell perform the Clearing Ritual, and take a few moments to feel the energy flowing down from the Sky and feeding up into you from the Earth. When you have cast out and cleansed your surroundings, you may begin.

Hold your Athame or wand before you (a hand gesture will suffice if in a public situation) and visualise a pure glowing green pentagram. Trace its points and draw it in the air ahead. As you do this, speak the following words;

> *Goddess of Light, and God of Might,*
> *Always At My Side, Through Any Plight,*
> *The elements before me, the elements behind me,*
> *I ask you all to Protect Me in this My Hour of Need!*
> *So Mote It Be.*

As you say the words stab the centre of the pentagram with your Athame, Wand or finger. This action radiates from the Pentagram circles of green energy which completely surround you and protect you, from in front to behind your back, above your head to below your feet. You are safe and under the Goddesses protection.

Mentally thank the Goddess and the God, and, when you feel that you are able perform a Grounding ritual. This 'turns down' your protective sphere, and returns you to your normal state.

Printed in Great Britain
by Amazon.co.uk, Ltd.,
Marston Gate.